D0590778

3641

THE LIBRARY
TOWER HAMLETS COLLEGE
JUBILEE STREET
LONDON E1 3HA
TEL: 071 538 5888

THE LIBRARY
CITY AND EAST LONDON COLLEGE
JUBILEE STREET, E1 3HA

TOWER HAMLETS COLLEGE

039289

GUSTAV KLIMT

L. SCHMIDT

GUSTAV KLIMT

THE LIBRARY
CITY AND EAST LONDON COLLEGE
JUBILEE STREET, E1 3HA

Artline Editions

THE LIBRARY
TOWER HAMLETS COLLEGE
JUBILEE STREET
LONDON E1 3HA
TEL. 071 538 5268

STL
759.36 KLI
039289

Translated by Stephen Gorman

Photographic acknowledgements:

ArtotHek J. Hinrichs, Planegg: 29, 57, 81, 93, 107
Bildarchiv A. Koch, München: 71, 105
Istituto Fotografico SCALA, Antella: 55, 97
Galerie Welz, Salzburg / Galerie Würthle, Wien /
Graphische Sammlung Albertina, Wien / Historisches
Museum, Wien.

© 1988 by Berghaus Verlag — D 8347 Kirchdorf/Inn
English Language Rights: Artlines UK Ltd, 1 Castle Street,
Thornbury, Bristol. Avon, England
Printed in West Germany — Imprimé en Allemagne
ISBN 1 871487 06 4

CONTENTS

ORIGIN AND EARLY YEARS

In Vienna around 1900, the work of Gustav Klimt was the artistic signal for the start into the 20th century. He was undeniably the most important Austrian artist in those years at the turn of the century, which led all over Europe to a complex art, an art whose aim was new and revolutionary contents of picture. Klimt's work developed continuously from the historiated view of the period of promoterism to a partly lively, partly static world of Art Nouveau which was highly decorative, till in his late work he eventually found access to an expressionistic form. A long way for an artist, particularly since none of his fellow companions were able to follow him for longer than one episode. His life is an exemplary illustration of the virtually compulsive development of a great artistic personality.

Klimt was born in an artistically quiet and comparatively unproductive time. The great ideas of the revolution in the romantic movement had been suffocated by the dogged, gruelling regulations of the all-controlling authorities. A middle-class style of painting which was satisfied with an increasing rise in splendour and pomp was dominant.

Gustav Klimt was born in 1863 in Baumgarten, a rural suburb of Vienna, the son of a gold engraver. He was the second of seven children. His father came from Bohemia and had worked his way from humble origins to a reasonably modest trade. His mother also came from a poor family. In her youth she had had ambitions for a career as a singer in the theatre without ever being able to realize that dream.

There was, however, a certain artistic creativity in the family. Gustav and two of his brothers were talented, and there were people who recognized this artistic skill and endeavoured to promote it. Artistic training was a concern of the government. Around 1876, the arts and crafts college of the Austrian Museum of Art and Industry had been founded. Gustav Klimt received a grant in 1876 which enabled him to study in this establishment. Later his brothers Ernst and Georg were also to attend this school. Gustav Klimt remained at the college for seven years. He was able to work practically during his training together with his brother Ernst and with Franz Matsch, a fellow student. Ferdinand Laufberger, their communal tutor, allowed them to help with the execution of the sgraffito work in the courtyards of the Museum for the History of Art in Vienna.

In 1880, Ferdinand Laufberger entrusted the three young artists with the creation of the four ceiling paintings in the Palais Sturany, obtained commissions for theatre decorations for them, and had them paint the central ceiling picture in the kurhaus in Karlsbad.

At that time, the whole of Vienna was under the spell of the prevalent artist Hans Makart. He was the only painter of this era in Austria who was acknowledged outside his country. The first years of Gustav Klimt's career were closely connected with Makart. The first direct contact came about when Makart staged a

gigantic pageant of unknown splendour in honour of the Ringstrasse boulevard after the erection of the first buildings there. The brothers Klimt and Franz Matsch were also among the contributors. Klimt first received smaller commissions from Makart and later was given complete ceiling paintings to execute.

The editor Martin Gerlach published – according to the tast of that time – the collected edition *Allegories and Emblems* in the style of the historical painting. Gustav Klimt received commissions for the preparation of several motifs for this collection of patterns. Together with his brother and Franz Matsch he was increasingly entrusted with the creation of decorative paintings on buildings, for example for the Rumanian royal palace in Pelesch, situated in the forest near Sinaia.

Eventually, Gustav and Ernst Klimt together with Franz Matsch were able to establish their own studio. Their style was in unison with their great ideal and master Hans Makart. All three appeared to be talented decorative artists, a trade which was in great demand due to the prevailing taste. In 1885, they were commissioned to paint the murals for the Hermes villa in Lainz from sketches by Makart; also in that year they carried out paintings for the theatre in Fiume. Before the pictures were erected there, they were shown in Vienna where they were well received by the general public. 1886 brought the decisive breakthrough for the studio. The young artists were commissioned to ornament the Karlsbad city theatre. Gustav Klimt painted the two large ceiling paintings; together they created the sensational curtain which was still based on a design by Makart. Makart had died in 1884.

Hans Makart's influence and significance cannot be estimated too highly. He was undeniably the master of the age, his style set the fashion, his enormous picture compositions were always a sensation as soon as they were shown to the public. The *Makart style* went beyond the scope of painting. It was a clear-cut concept in the decoration of living rooms and stages, in fashion and in the arts and crafts. It was due to Makart that in the period of promoterism the imperial Vienna was able to dominate the upper-class flats, even as far as the Paris salons. "A lifestyle, which was only reserved to the clergy and the nobility until the French revolution, now began to form a luxurious middle-class society in the German speaking nations as well. Unpretentiousness and strictness, which had still determined the standard of living in the Biedermeier period, were considered

more and more as backwardness and narrowness. The need for representation now arose with an increasing self-confidence also in regard to graphic art. Makart delivered the required spectacle with his giant historical paintings. He offered an illusion which confused the senses and satisfied the demands of the affluent society. The historical action only offered him the opportunity to show decoration in a great style in an historiated guise: splendour and pomp, precious materials in an artistic draping, luxurious pageantry, and last but not least voluptuous nakedness in a languorous interpretation which appealed to sensuality. He directed his attention right from the beginning to the splendour of colour, glowing luminous hues with which he achieved splendid results. Makart's fame was enhanced because he surrounded himself with a secretive aura and because he knew how to play the role of the master artist who had been raised to a noble position. The magnificent parties in his studio which was fitted out with the most extravagant splendour belonged to the most fashionable occasions. He persistently influenced the taste of leading society whose steep rise to a short period of luxury and good living was already overshadowed by the coming of social revolutions. Makart's studio and his decorative art delivered the ideal model for living rooms, luxuriously decorated with draperies." (Tolzien)

Gustav Klimt had received his artistic training in the sphere of Makart's influence, during his period of learning he worked in the style of the Grand Master of the Belle Epoque. "It is understandable that the young Klimt was drawn away from the intimate and led towards large areas, to a decorative style of painting and its connection with architecture." (Max Eisler) In the following years, however, his attitude towards art underwent a change. What remained was a preference for sumptuous scenes, for the grand gesture. Klimt's artistic personality emanated from the Makart style. If he had not developed in his own direction, he could have remained an excellent successor to the master. But Klimt changed his work constantly, developed with his tasks, and realized his own artistic aims. He consequently restricted himself more and more to the essentials in his paintings. But no matter how much he condensed his paintings, the large forms – absorbed by his inner self – remained his heritage of Makart. Even his drawings, pencilled with very fine lines, countless sketches of women, always had a very strong static moment. He never tried to capture movement in an impressionistic manner. He superelevated the instant to eternity, the gesture became for ever valid.

The zenith of Gustav Klimt's career as a historical painter was a commission for the Burgtheater in Vienna: he created the ceiling and lunette paintings for both the stairways. The completion of this work brought him the highest acknowledgement: Emperer Franz Joseph awarded him the Golden Cross.

But this was the last work with which Klimt was accepted in court and in the awareness of the general public. From now on, Klimt's artistic aims moved in a way which excluded them from a favourable acceptance by the masses. Although the studio of the three former fellow students Gustav Klimt and Ernst Klimt as well as Franz Matsch functioned well in the daily tasks and development of the large public commissions, one should not overlook the fact that the three artists developed noticeably away from each other during those years. Gustav Klimt's artistic will forced him towards new aims. It began with an increased analysis of the stylistic elements of Impressionism, with attempts to insert light as a decisive compositional characteristic into his paintings. At the end of the decade, Klimt turned completely away from the academic conception of pictures. The paintings which he carried out for his next major commission were already very different from the works of both his studio colleagues. This assignment was to complete the decoration in the staircase of the Museum for the History of Art in Vienna, another task which the studio had taken over from the heritage of Hans Makart. The figures which Gustav Klimt painted were presented in a strict frontality in in front of a golden background. They made clear the stylistic change of the artist. The good execution of the work and the favourable resonance from the public made the authorities consider the studio for the design of the university hall as well. At the end of the year, however, there was a far-reaching change. Ernst Klimt suddenly died. He had been the binding link between the other two artists, since Matsch always remained stylistically attracted to a conservative style of decoration. The studio received the commission in spite of Ernst Klimt's death, and Matsch presented the complete plan for the decoration of the university hall. The artists were commissioned to prepare the final sketches for the individual paintings. This project was not just an artistic challenge for Gustav Klimt which occupied him for many years. The adverse conditions of the external execution also put a great strain on him and soured years of his life.

The board of the Viennese Academy of Fine Arts proposed Gustav Klimt for the professorship of the historical painting section. To the great amazement of the board, however, the emperor appointed someone else.

KLIMT'S YEARS IN THE VIENNA SECESSION

In the years before the turn of the century Vienna's artists were organized in the *Genossenschaft bildender Künstler Wien* (Fellowship of Graphic Artists in Vienna), the so-called artists' fellowship. In March 1897, a group of younger members who were dissatisfied with the encrusted structures of the society decided to establish their own alliance within the fellowship. They called themselves *Vienna Secession*, and their aim was a reform of the artistic life and a change in the nature of exhibitions in favour of the impulse of modernism. The artistic leader of the group was Gustav Klimt. He also informed the artists' fellowship committee and the press of the new foundation and explained the aims. Forty names were on the list of the founder members. Klimt became president and Rudolf von Alt honorary president. The foundation of the Secession was regarded as a challenge by the mainly conservative members of the artists' fellowship. It came to a dramatic meeting during which Gustav Klimt and several comrades-in-arms got up and left the hall. Two days later, the Secession artists declared their resignation from the artists' fellowship and constituted themselves in the new association, now as an independent artists' organization.

They imagined a lively exhibition activity. Their dissatisfaction with the exhibition possibilities had been one of the main reasons which had led to the formation of the Secession. Klimt sketched a design for an exhibition building with the inscription *VER SACRUM, Vereinigung bildender Künstler Österreichs* (Association of Graphic Artists in Austria), but there was still a very long way before such a building could be realized. The outside enclosure for an exhibition was very important to the young artists, since they were convinced that paintings needed suitable surroundings to achieve their effect. The complete work of art was the visionary aim, an organic whole of building, furnishings, and exhibited objects. A nail in the wall was certainly not sufficient.

In the initial enthusiasm, a magazine for the publication of art and literature was planned and was actually published under the title *VER SACRUM, Sacred Springtime*. Because of its considerable significance also for Gustav Klimt's work, it is sensible to give it a separate chapter in this book.

There were a long way from having their own house, but as exhibitions were to be organized as soon as possible, it was decided to rent space for the first exhibition of the Secession in the house of the horticultural society on the Parkring. They made intensive efforts to encourage a lively participation of foreign artists, especially French modern artists, in order to bring Vienna out of its isolation. In fact, works were displayed from Böcklin, Carrière, Mucha, Puvis de Chavannes, Khnopff, Meunier, and Rodin, and the exhibition was received very well by the public. Klimt's displayed works were well acknowledged. There was trouble with the design of the placard which was by Klimt. Although the Theseus wore a fig leaf in a certain place because of lack of clothing, the poster was condemned as indecent. Trees which were printed on later covered the incriminating part sufficiently to make the poster acceptable.

 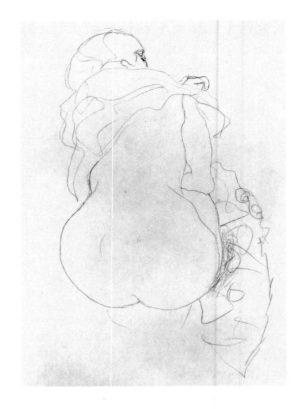

In 1898, Klimt had to present the design for the faculty paintings in the university hall to the art commission of the Ministry of Education. With his sketches for 'Law' and 'Philosophy', it was mainly formal reasons which led to criticism. But his design for 'Medicine' was criticized because of its liberal arrangement. Especially the left female figure, conceived as a symbol for suffering humanity, was objected to, and its replacement by a more decently fashioned male figure was recommended. Klimt threatened to withdraw from the contract if he was not allowed any scope for the artistic creation. The chairman of the commission eventually succeeded in having the design accepted by his committee with small alterations as "within the limits drawn by the protection of artistic freedom".

On the whole, the struggle about the faculty paintings was a gruelling chapter for Klimt, and the public also found the squabbling unpleasant. Ludwig Hevesi wrote: "Not to receive any public commissions is fatal for an artist, but the opposite seems to be even more vexing. And then comes the mockery of fate, the artist has to answer for that which has been forced on him in the commissional civil wars."

The new Secession building took form. An edifice, planned by Joseph Maria Olbrich, was erected. It embraced the beliefs of the young artists in stone. "Because of this it was regarded as a typical Art Nouveau building in Vienna. It brings together all the characteristics of that particular form of Viennese Art Nouveau which is called *Secessionism*. The geometric character, which distinguishes it in a special way, is already apparent in this early structure, although later it becomes more decisively obvious in other examples. It consists of characteristic geometric basic forms, cubes, squares, spheres. On the other hand, the ornamental decoration was used with the greatest economy, something which was future orientated; the decoration does not cover or affect the main form of the building in any way, it rather more underlines it visually." (Waissenberger)

The second Secession exhibition, now in the new house, contained among other works from Klimt his *Pallas Athene* which brought him strong criticism. On the other hand, he achieved great success with his painting *Franz Schubert am Klavier*, which he had created for the Palais of Dumba but which he displayed beforehand in an exhibition. The works of other artists received very different reactions from the public as well. In the third Secession exhibition in January 1899, Max Klinger's painting *Christus im Olymp* took a central position, and the public expressed a great dislike for it. In the same exhibition, one could also view the pointillist work of Theo van Rysselberghe. Gustav Klimt also experimented at that time with the pointillist technique, for example in several landscapes and his painting *Nuda Veritas*. To this painting he attached Schiller's motto: "If you cannot please everyone with your actions and your art — please a few. It is not good to please too many."

The 7th exhibition of the Secession experienced large crowds of people. Klimt displayed his painting *Philosophy* with the appendage "incomplete". Beside this, he exhibited his first landscapes.

The years between 1900 and 1904 were characterized by repeated discussions with critics, public, and the authorities. It started with an appeal by eleven professors to their colleagues to prevent the mounting of the painting *Philosophy* in the festivity hall of the university. The board of the Secession immediately protested to the Ministry of Education against this interference. Nevertheless it came to a petition against the painting, signed by 87 members of the professorship. The artistic advisor in the ministry remained firm. The petition was refused.

The Secession sent almost as many paintings to the world exhibition in Paris as the artists' fellowship which had a great deal more members. Klimt's contribution was especially stressed in the official French catalogue, the painting *Philosophy* received the gold medal for the best foreign painting. This decision was even more surprising when one remembers the artistic expressions from French studios which determined the official standards.

In the 10th Secession exhibition, Gustav Klimt eventually showed the painting *Medicine*. The press criticized him scathingly. The public also turned against the painting to a great extent. However, attendance of the exhibition went beyond all scope. The public prosecutor applied for the seizure of the magazine VER SACRUM in which the studies for the painting had been published. The responsible court of justice, however, refused this: "It surely does not have to be mentioned that the artist, in respect to the objects of his imagination as well as in respect to the execution of his artistic ideas cannot have limits drawn, or that the representation of naked forms — which has existed as long as art — should be forbidden. It would not be proper in all cases where we are dealing with a serious work of art, meaning that it exists for a purely aesthetic interest, to talk about injuring morals or modesty." Conservative members of parliament attacked Klimt's work vehemently, but the minister decisively refused to interfere. Klimt

himself, his lifelong taciturn as regards statements about his artistic situation, reacted with a short explanation in the *Wiener Morgenzeitung*: "I do not have the time to involve myself personally in this argument. I find it too stupid, time and time again, to stand up against the same stubborn people – when I have completed a painting I do not want to waste months, defending it to the whole populace. It does not interest me how many like it, but rather who likes it."

On the other hand, Hermann Bahr, a critical author, gave a lecture which was well acknowledged and which was significant beyond the daily topicalities. "... then it is my opinion that this is not the time to have a pleasant conversation as long as the Klimt case has not been settled and this attack on art has not been warded off. I do not want to defend Klimt. Thank God he really does not need that, not he nor his work ... he has the wonderful confidence of the great whose path is determined by an inner law. They cannot lose faith because they are content with themselves. It is not he who is threatened, rather it is us. Nothing can happen to him, but we will become the laughing stock of Europe." Bahr attacked the supposedly injured aesthetic feelings of the majority of the public, a charge made in parliament in a fiery speech: "No, Sir, you are wrong: art does not exist to suit the moods of your majority! Art always existed to express the aesthetic feelings of a minority of noble-minded, superior, and more exquisite people from whom the reluctant, slow masses eventually shall learn what is beautiful and good." The painting *Medicine* was also shown at the 8th International Art Exhibition in Munich where it was at the most acknowledged without attracting any great interest.

The board of professors of the Academy of Fine Art attempted anew to have the most famous Austrian painter appointed as professor. But again in vain: the royal court decided against Klimt, he was passed over again. It is not recorded how much this humiliation affected or impressed Klimt. Another event, however, which was very important for his work was a journey which Klimt undertook with the painter Maximilian Lenz. It led him to the Byzantine frescoes in Upper Italy. Wilhelm Dessauer described the memorable tour: "By moon-light one travels through the valley of the Po estuary. Ravenna, the actual destination is reached: Gustav Klimt's moment of destiny has arrived. The golden shimmering

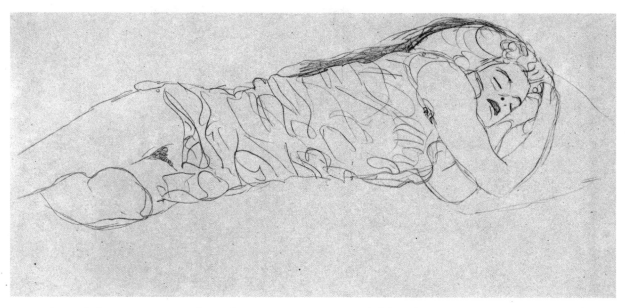

mosaics of the Ravenna churches make an incredible, decisive impression on him. From then on, the resplendance and the rigid-magnificent appears in his sensitive art. Lenz tells us: Klimt was really deeply moved. He did not say anything, but one saw it clearly."

The merit of the Secession by introducing foreign artists to the Viennese cannot be rated highly enough in those years. The 12th Secession exhibition showed, for example, apart from important works from Hodler, paintings from Edvard Munch and Jan Toorop for whom the magazine VER SACRUM issued a separate edition.

In the 14th exhibition, the Secession realized for the first time the attempt to create a symbolical complete work of art. Works which were connected with the theme were grouped around Max Klinger's Beethoven statue. Gustav Klimt's contribution was the Beethoven frieze which at the same time can be regarded as the peak in the development of Viennese Art Nouveau. The following summary of the frieze was printed in the catalogue: "First long wall opposite the entrance: the ardent desire for happiness. The suffering of a weak humanity: its entreaties to the well-equipped powerful as external, compassion and ambition as inner driving forces, which move them to take up the struggle for happiness. Short wall: the enemy powers. The giant Typhoeus, against whom even the gods fought in vain: his daughters, the three Gorgons. Sickness, madness, death. Lust and Immodesty, inttemperance. Gnawing worries. The longings and wishes of the people fly over and away. Second long wall: the desire for happiness finds appeasement in poetry. The arts lead us over to the ideal realm where we are able to find pure happiness, pure joy, pure love. The choir of angels of paradise, joy — thou spark of flame immortal. This kiss for the world!" Felix Salten reported from the preliminary viewing: "It was two days before the exhibition. The last and final touches were being put to the works in the various halls. But already there were a few visitors in the house, journalists, art patrons, the curious. It was the typical time before an opening. Klimt was still painting on his scaffold in a corner of the left hall in front of his frescoes. Klimt painted, stood close to the ceiling in a blue smock which had embroidery under the arm, done by a female hand. He was engrossed in his work and did not notice the people who walked through the room below and accepted the newness of his latest work with their

comments. His colleagues left him in peace. 'He is still painting!' they told the visitors in the same way as one says, 'he is asleep'. With their fingers on their lips. Those who saw him standing up there, completely absorbed in his painting, as if in his own atmosphere, isolated from the others, talked quieter and kept their critical comments to themselves. So that the judgement was not ready before the work which at that moment was being completed. Suddenly someone called from the middle of the hall 'dreadful!' and ran out before one had registered exactly what had happened. An aristocratic patron and collector had become so insulting in the face of Klimt's frescoes. He shouted the word with his high, shrill, piercing voice as if someone had pinched him. He threw the word up against the wall like a stone. 'Dreadful!' Everyone started and stared at the fleeing figure with uncomprehending, shocked, and angry faces. Klimt had also heard the cry. He turned round, moved to the edge of the scaffold and looked down – really looked down – on the fleeing count. And he had an expression on his face as if looking at a child who has behaved in an all too human way in the middle of a room – taken aback, amused, and at the same time forgiving."

The comprehension of the art of the Impressionists and the acceptance of the close connections, common sources, and many parallels between the post-

Impressionists and the former Impressionists was not as widespread anywhere else outside France as in Vienna. Without doubt, the art patrons in the metropolis on the Danube were so excellently informed mainly by the exhibition activities of the Secession. Above all, the Impressionist exhibition in 1903 was of the highest quality. In the exhibition a comprehensive view of this great era of French painting was given with the inclusion of Vuillard, Bonnard, van Gogh and Cézanne, Gauguin and Toulouse-Lautrec. It showed the continuity between the Impressionists and these succeeding artists. The Viennese exhibition had a considerable influence on the understanding of contemporary artists, and painters such as Klimt were obviously able to place certain impressionistic areas of their work in a larger context. When, three years later, the Gallery Miethke presented a van Gogh exhibition, it was quite obvious how strong van Gogh's stages of development were reflected in Klimt's work.

The old demand from the early days of the English Arts and Crafts movement, namely to allow the independent arts a close co-operation with the crafts, also found a place in the endeavours of the Vienna Secession group. Josef Hoffmann and Koloman Moser gave new impulse to the art life in Vienna with the foundation of the Wiener Werkstätte. An aspiring small colony of artist craftsmen arose within a short time, energetically supported by Klimt. The determining power and artistic potency of Gustav Klimt were evident in the activities of the Wiener Werkstätte.

In November 1903, the arts commission of the Ministry of Culture planned to view the faculty paintings by Gustav Klimt. In the following meeting, where the paintings were, on the whole, positively accepted, the opinion was formed that the paintings should be mounted in the Gallery of Modern Art and not, as originally planned, in the university hall, as the difference in quality between the conservative decoration from Franz Matsch and the progressive paintings by Klimt was too noticeable.

Repeated attacks on the faculty paintings had the effect that Klimt became obviously angry which eventually led in 1905 to him writing a letter, resigning from the contract and returning the advance payments which he had already received. At first the ministry did not want to do without the paintings, in the course of a larger dispute, however, it did eventually come to the settlement which had been proposed by Klimt. It left a deeply injured artist and a minister who resigned from his post.

The Academy of Fine Art again proposed Klimt's appointment as professor. This appointment would in fact have been long overdue, as Klimt had long been regarded in the rest of the world as the most significant Viennese artist of the era around the turn of the century, but again it was hindered by forces in the royal court.

Within the Secession, there was increasing tension. A number of group members was not prepared to allow artistic freedom. Finally, when Carl Moll, who was the artistic adviser for the Gallery Miethke, was attacked by these circles for his liberal allocation practise, it came to the break: Gustav Klimt and his friends resigned from the Secession.

VER SACRUM

"We want a form of art which is not servile to foreigners, but which is not afraid of nor hates outside influence. Foreign art should inspire us to reflect upon ourselves, we want to acknowledge it if it is worthy of our admiration; we just do not want to copy it."

The magazine *Jugend*, which gave its name to "Jugendstil" (Art Nouveau), was regarded for a long time as the fundamental publishing authority for the new art at the turn of the century. Its consistent involvement with style and the wide distribution of its large number of copies ensured for this classification. In reality, however, the journal was unmistakably drawn to a certain simplicity and shallowness, its niveau was that of a widely circulated boulevard paper, which in fact it was.

Much more serious in its artistic ambitions, however, was *Pan*, a magazine which emanated from the Berlin Bohemians. It was conceived in the wine-tavern *Zum schwarzen Ferkel*, where a group of mainly Scandinavian artists congregated around August Strindberg. Edvard Munch also belonged to this circle as did Otto Julius Bierbaum, who was one of the founders of the magazine together with Julius Meier-Graefe. The last two also edited the first editions of the magazine. One had imagined a liberal co-existence of various art directions as the basis of the magazine, and in the beginning proved to be open-minded. However, a lithograph from Henri de Toulouse-Lautrec which was printed in the magazine was sufficient to deprive the editors of their posts. The sponsors of the magazine came from Germany's high finance, and they were not prepared to put up with a "flash of colour, lace, sneering, shouting, impudence". Meier-Graefe who was affected described the litho in question with these words. Pan was convincing in its set-up, it was of a superior quality and relatively modern – and in spite of these provisions had to be discontinued after five years. Malicious rumours said that the last subscriber had passed away peacefully after this time ...

In 1891 in France, *La Revue Blanche*, the magazine founded by the brothers Nathanson, became the mouthpiece of the *Nabis*. Felix Valloton, one of the central figures in the development of modern graphics at once helped *Revue Blanche* to great recognition. Also Beardsley and William Nicholson were decisively influenced by his contributions in the magazine. The quality and seriousness of *Pan* and *La Revue Blanche* were undoubtedly the ideal when the plans for an art magazine were being discussed in Vienna in the circle of the newly founded Secession. Certainly one had *Jugend* with its chic layout there, but one wanted to make a magazine which was discriminating in regards to graphics and content. *VER SACRUM* was conceived, and for the opening a *foundation edition* was presented, a luxuriously designed special edition which was very expensive. It was intended to supply the means for the running of the magazine. They did without a publisher except for a few editions and mainly brought out the magazine themselves under their own management. The preface to the first edition was a fundamental manifesto: "Our aim is to awaken the feelings of our

time for art, to inspire and to spread these feelings," the editors wrote in their programme. "... it is up to us to lead the way. You may depend on our allegiance, we have dedicated all our power and future and everything that we are to a sacred springtime."

The author Ludwig Hevesi accompanied the Secession artists through all the years of their activity with alert interest and noticeable benevolence. He welcomed the appearance of VER SACRUM warmly. "Together with the young year, the first number of VER SACRUM has been inssued, the mouthpiece of the union of graphic artists in Austria. It has been the subject of daily conversation for a long time, has brought pleasure to some and annoyance to others ... A glance at this first copy of the new art magazine and one sees, here is an artist who knows what he wants ... These young people are idealists. They want to show on paper to those who have had enough of the stereotype art that there is something new to see, something which has just grown up ... All in all, we regard the artistic success as unquestionable. A start has been made and evidence produced. Ver

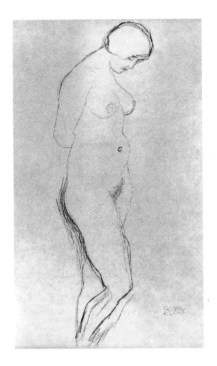

Sacrum has in many places exceeded the expectations. Nothing similar has been attempted in Vienna, and now a cloud of doubt has been scattered ... The magazine has a high artistic value because of this. It was much criticized in the beginning, even mocked, while Paris, London, Munich, and America immediately recognized the sincerity of their endeavours and accepted the accomplishment as such. Today, Ver Sacrum has been recognized as a leading authority for modern art. Not because of its theorizing, it does not occupy itself much with this, but because of the example which it gives. *The sacred spring of consecration* and similar terms have been mocked, but no one dares to deny anymore that the Secession really has brought spring to Viennese art. Ver Sacrum becomes more valuable and richer in contents with every new issue ..."

Gustav Klimt was undoubtedly the most important personality in the circle of artists connected with Ver Sacrum. He did not form a school, did not take any pupils, no artist followed in his wake; he remained an individualist. However, all of his artist friends were convinced of his outstanding artistic leadership and his ungrudging support for young artists who found different ways to the artistic development of their personality; this made him a revered example. His commitment to the magazine was considerable, numerous sketches and also a number of works especially prepared for the magazine were published.

The magazine was relatively reserved in respect to contributions about foreign artists. Although the Secession was very open-minded to artists from other countries and brought them into their exhibitions in great profusion, the magazine Ver Sacrum was seen above all as an organ for the artists from the group; a mouthpiece for the young Austrian artists. "Ver Sacrum gave — apart from the triumvirate Josef Hoffmann, Gustav Klimt, Koloman Moser, and a short guest performance from Maria Olbrich — an amazingly large amount of young Austrian artists the possibility to co-operate. They achieved excellent results." (G. Nebehay)

GREATNESS BRINGS LONELINESS

"It is our opinion that in view of the tremendous change of all conceptions the artists should not just limit their activities to the occasional arrangement of exhibitions, but that they should endeavour to attain more and more influence on the manifestations of modern life; they are in fact obliged to use every available opportunity to promote the arts in their widest sense and to convince increasing numbers of people that no life is so rich that it cannot become richer through art, none so poor that there would be no place for art in it." This fundamental statement was written by young artists in the circle around Gustav Klimt in an open letter to the Ministry of Education when they decided to resign from the Secession. They justified their withdrawal from the Secession with this letter. The progressive powers around Klimt felt it necessary to declare their position beyond controversial points of the workaday routine in the artistic life. Klimt himself undoubtedly suffered from his own speechlessness. He was completely committed to the life of an artist, constantly in discord with the daily cultural-political events, and hardly ever found the way to a clarifying statement. It is not recorded how far the statements from the group were made with his active involvement. Certainly among the great literary figures who were his friends there were enough eloquent fighters for a new free art.

A considerable part of Klimt's work consists of the innumerable fine sketches, precious documents of a splendid artistry, about which Hermann Bahr once wrote, "The last secret was revealed to him: the art of leaving out everything which was unnecessary. His hand had become like a divining-rod, he let it glide silently along the world's illusion until it twitchingly told him where some essence was buried; these sketches of his mastership are shortened reports of such divinations for the well of appearance. His eye had almost been blinded by the inferno of the conception of appearance, now his hand listened to the origins: in-between is the common plainness of the day, this he had never used."

Klimt drew quickly and painted infinitely slowly. His works include many thousands of sketches but only just over two hundred paintings.

"What does Klimt draw? It is almost always female nudes. He never tires of recording the lineal flow of the pelvis, the melodic rhythm of a hip, or the soft roundness of a shoulder in gentle lines. It is really wonderful how he converts his sensitive feeling into an artistic idea with lascivious sensuality. The word of Sar Peladan surely relates to these works: spiritual sketching, soulful lines, felt form — you embody our dreams." (Richard Muther)

While the paintings play the programmatic part in Klimt's work, the sketches are evidence of the artistic quality. The paintings often brought something new: new intellectual themes, new forms of rhythmics, new colours. Klimt's masterly achievement in the great stream of the history of art becomes apparent in his painting. "He did not see a road before him, even less an aim, he only felt a direction; that of his feeling. Through the middle of an immeasurable territory, already furrowed with hidden paths and stumbling blocks, also by several strongly defined military roads, along which other emotional artists strove. They did not have anything definite but the direction. One can never say: forwards; one can only say: anywhere, but not where they all came from. Away from that which lay behind this point. The hate of things eternally dismissed joined them together, made them brothers. Another thing; instead of the old herd a new herd. Klimt also had the strength to cast this off, to go well in advance of it, in the direction of his feeling, his inner experience of development: roots, corolla, blossom, fruit. At the moment it is still blossom; will it ever come to fruit? Never. Klimt is an artist in perpetual bloom, a part of the never-ending spring. These are the great primitives in art. They never achieve their purpose. L'art pour l'art only carries a meaning for them.'' (Ludwig Hevesi)

The Palais Stoclet was a great Art Nouveau building, committed to the concept of a complete work of art. Receiving the commission was a great moment for the artists. Around 1904, the young Belgian magnate Adolphe Stoclet approached the architect Josef Hoffmann and commissioned him to build a palais in Brussels which should be built and furnished in one single style. Stoclet tied absolutely no conditions to the commission and was prepared to pay the costs with no restrictions. A building of sensuous beauty was created, pure in its easy to survey, right-angled order. The human, harmonious proportions of the external building were carried forth in the interior. A generous sequence of rooms enabled optimal decoration. Hoffmann commissioned Klimt to decorate the dining-room, and so a universal work of art was created. It became a mutual peak in the artistic creativity of both. In 1907, Klimt altered the faculty paintings for the last time after which they were exhibited in the Gallery Miethke in Vienna and in Berlin.

Apart from the ordinary arts-and-crafts work in the Wiener Werkstätte, it came to an extension in the range of work: the cabaret *Fledermaus* was furnished. It became a meeting place for the stylists as the Klimt group was often called.

The first exhibition from the group was the *Kunstschau Wien 1908* which took place in a provisional building which had been erected by Josef Hoffmann. Klimt held the opening speech and exhibited 16 important pictures. The pièce de résistance of his presentation *The Kiss* was immediately bought by the Austrian National Gallery. The young Oskar Kokoschka made his exhibition début in the art show, and in the course of the preparations for the exhibition Klimt also met Egon Schiele with whom he became good friends a short time later. They had many mutual artistic points of contact. When one tried to warn Klimt of the high-flying expressionistic art of Egon Schiele and Oskar Kokoschka, he replied: "We are obliged to give a great talent the possibility of expression. Oskar Kokoschka is the greatest talent of the young generation. And even if we are in danger of having our art exhibition demolished, one can do nothing about it. But we have done our duty ..."

The Gallery Miethke began with the publication of the portfolio *The Work of Gustav Klimt*, and the critic Bertha Zuckerkandl published the book *Zeitkunst Wien* with several essays about Klimt.

In 1909, the second exhibition from the new group took place, entitled *Kunstschau 1909*. They used the same building as for the previous exhibition. After the second exhibition, it was demolished, and in its place the Vienna Concert House was later built. This second exhibition again contained important paintings from Klimt (who, by the way, officiated as president of the art show), but also paintings from van Gogh, Munch, Toorop, Gauguin, Valloton, and Matisse whose use of colours noticeably influenced Klimt. Work was begun on the Stoclet frieze for Brussels in the Wiener Werkstätte under Klimt's supervision. There were also many exhibitions and participation in exhibitions in other countries. If one reads reports from exhibitions from European cities from this time, the reviewer seldom forgets the reference to a picture by the Viennese artist Gustav Klimt which caused a sensation and which was regarded as a special document of the individual Viennese style. For example, Klimt was awarded first prize at the International Art Exhibition in Rome in 1911. Klimt took advantage of the mounting of the Stoclet frieze for a short stay in Brussels, then he visited London and Madrid.

In 1917, he received two honours. The Academy of Fine Art in Vienna, who in spite of many attempts to nominate him as professor were unable to enforce this against higher powers, appointed the artist as honourary member. The Academy of Graphic Art in Munich did the same. While the honour in Munich followed the custom that foreigners and non-artists who had earned merit in art could be honoured in this way, the recognition in his own country was filled with a certain embarrassment.

Gustav Klimt suffered a cerebral apoplexy at the end of a Christmas trip to Rumania in January 1918 and died after a few weeks. He left behind a rich life's work, varied and constantly changing with his restless search for new possibilities of expression. His work was the keystone of a great century of Austrian painting. He was allowed to carry the elements of this great time into a new century, into a new expressive art which soon moved away from Austria and became, as expressionism, the supporting force of European art of the 20th century.

ILLUSTRATIONS

Music I. 1895

Oil on canvas, 37 x 44.5 cm
Neue Pinakothek, Munich

Pallas Athene. 1898
Oil on canvas, 75 x 75 cm
Historisches Museum, Vienna

Portrait of Sonja Knips. 1898
Oil on canvas, 145 x 145 cm
Österreichische Galerie, Vienna

Nuda Veritas. 1899
Oil on canvas, 260 x 64.5 cm
Theatersammlung, Vienna

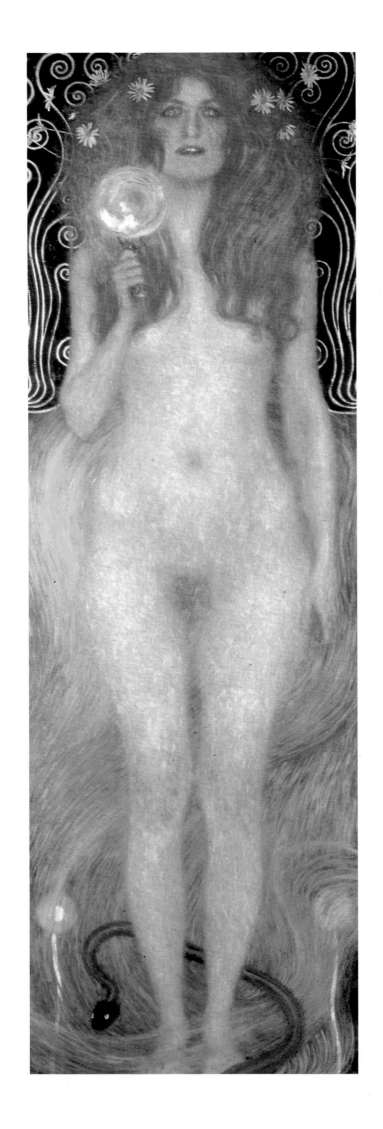

41

GVSTAV
KLIMT

Judith I. 1901
Oil on canvas, 84 x 42 cm
Österreichische Galerie, Vienna

Portrait of Emilie Flöge. 1902
Oil on canvas, 178 x 80 cm
Historisches Museum, Vienna

Birch Wood. 1903
Oil on canvas, 110 x 110 cm
Neue Galerie der Stadt Linz,
Wolfgang-Gurlitt-Museum

Water-Snakes I. 1904/07
Water-colour, 50 x 20 cm
Österreichische Galerie, Vienna

The Three Ages of Woman. 1905
Oil on canvas, 180 x 180 cm
Gall. Nazionale d'Arte Moderna, Rome

55

Garden with Sunflowers. 1905/06
Oil on canvas, 110 x 110 cm
Österreichische Galerie, Vienna

Margaret Stonborough-Wittgenstein. 1905
Oil on canvas, 180 x 80 cm
Neue Pinakothek, Munich

Garden with Sunflowers. 1905/06
Oil on canvas, 110 x 110 cm
Österreichische Galerie, Vienna

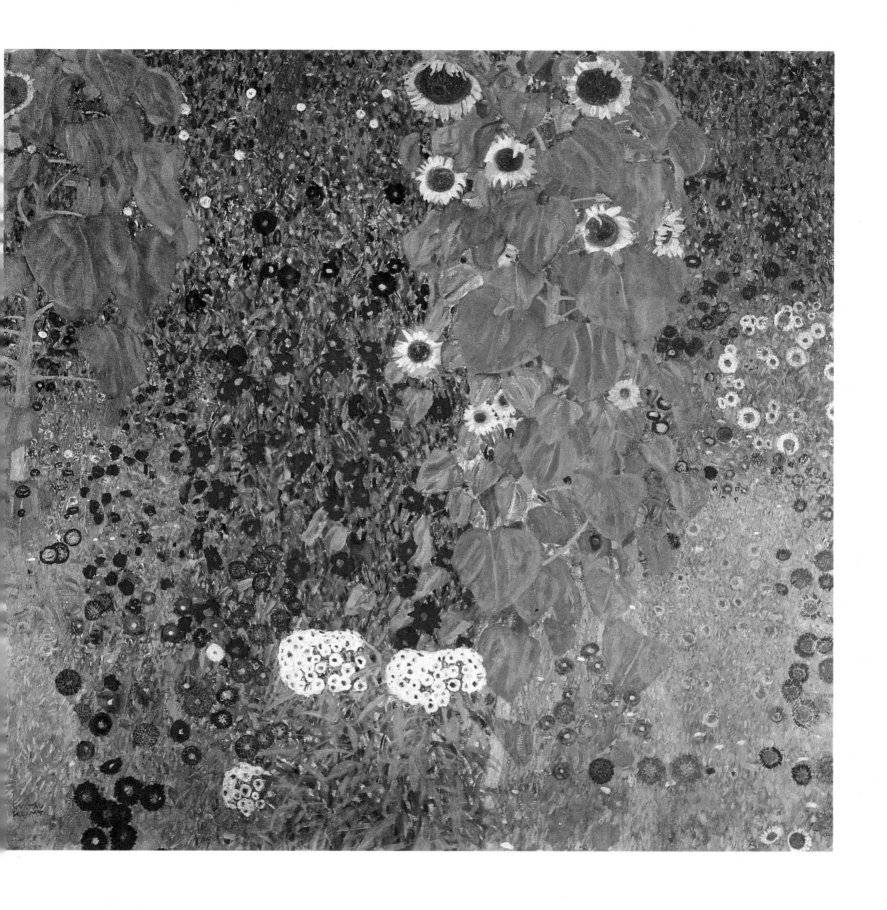

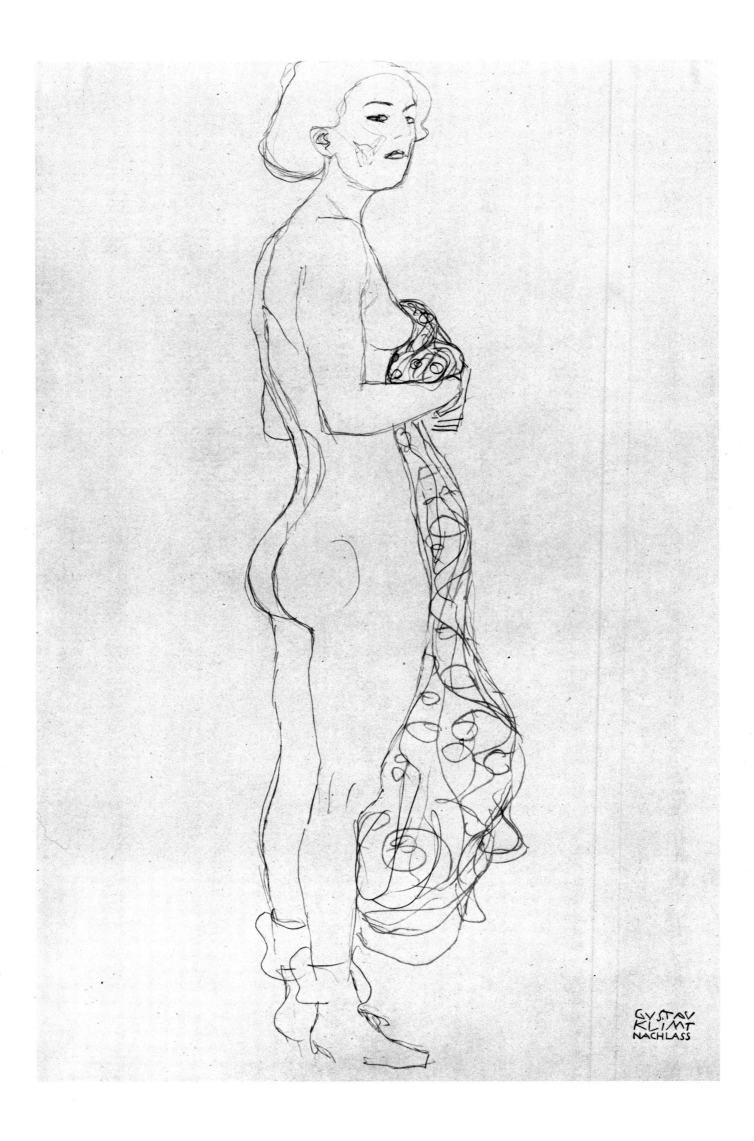

60

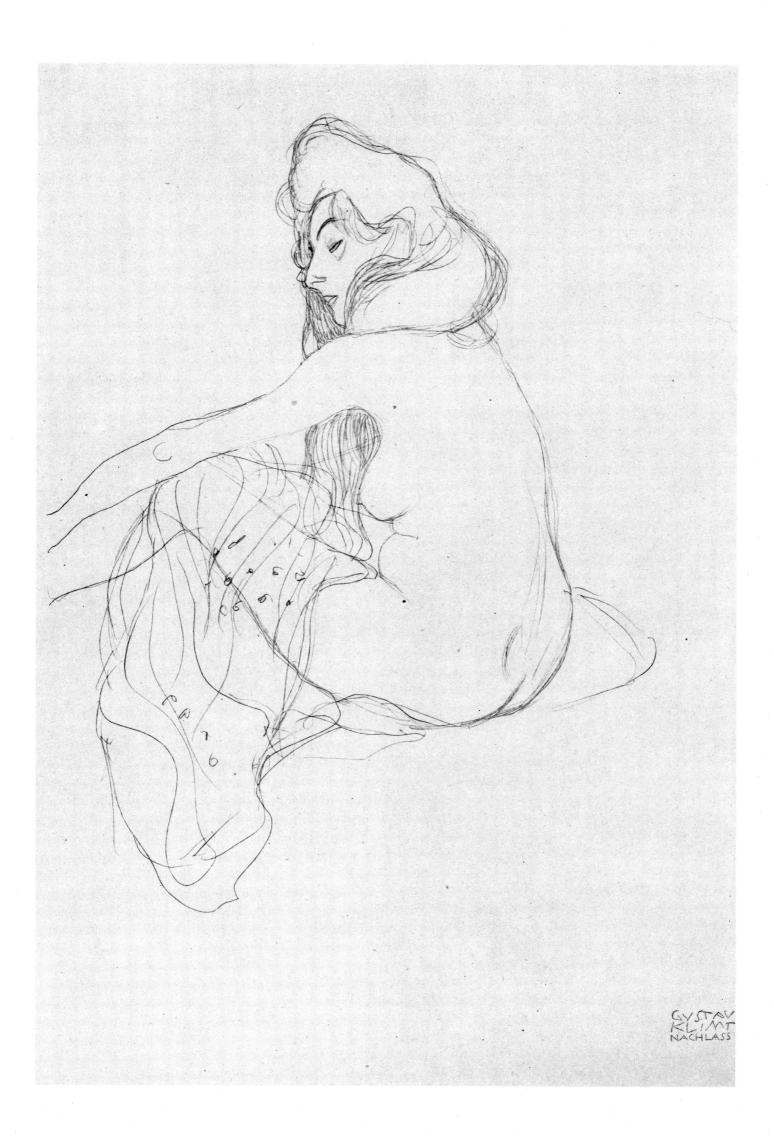

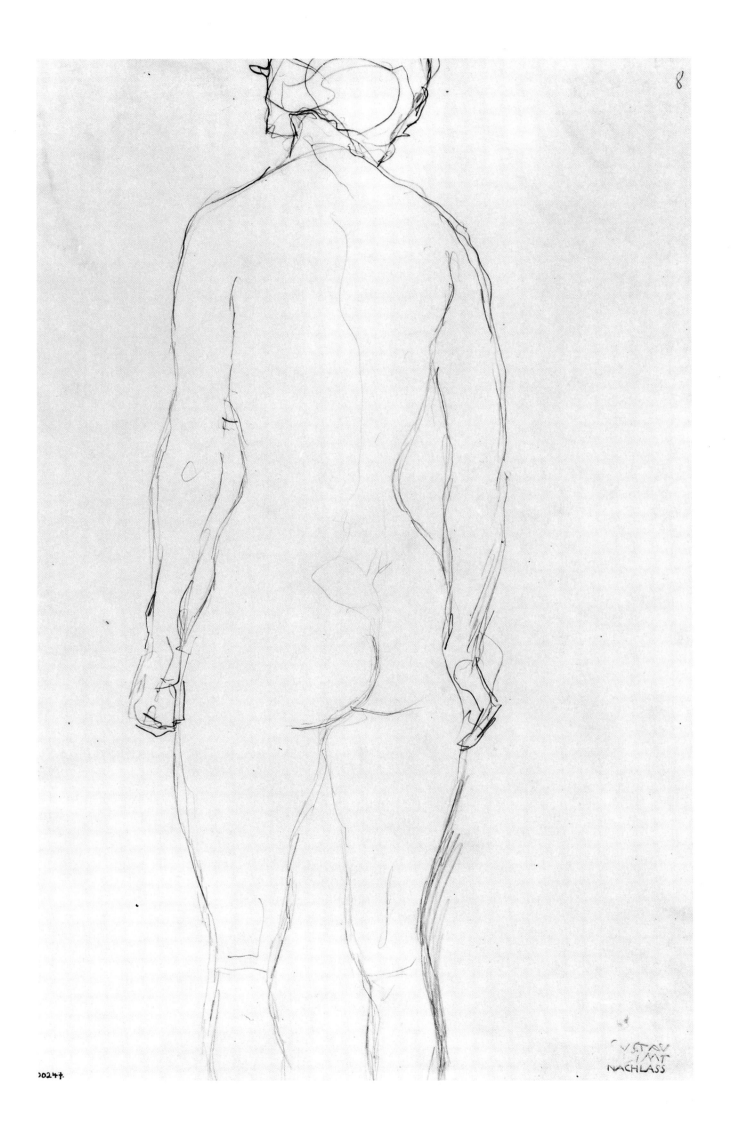

50247.

GVSTAV
KLIMT
NACHLASS

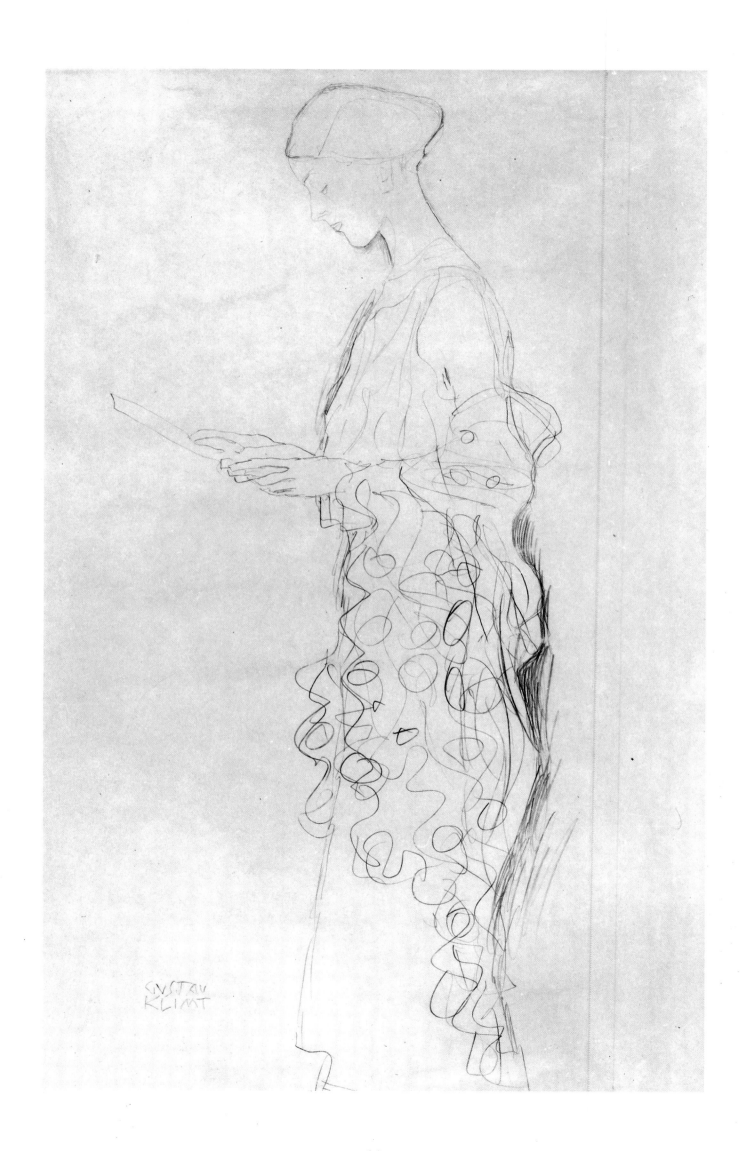

Portrait of Fritza Riedler. 1906
Oil on canvas, 153 x 153 cm
Österreichische Galerie, Vienna

Flower Garden. 1906/08
Oil on canvas, 110 x 110 cm
Narodny Galerie, Prague

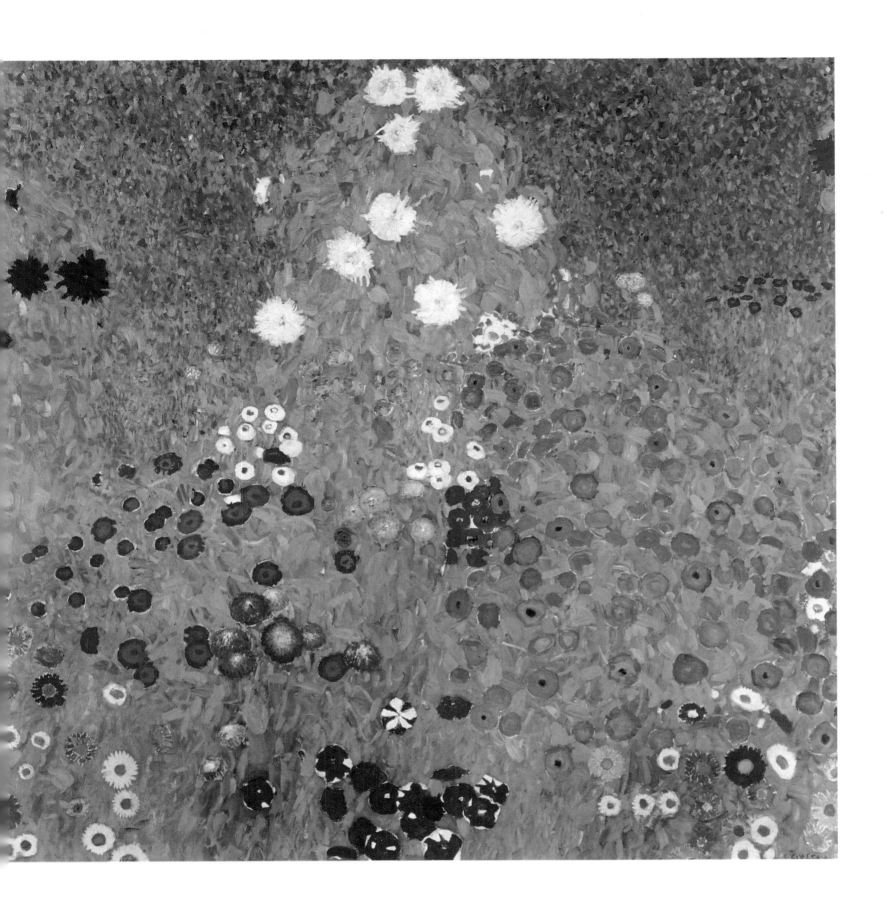

Poppy Field. 1907
Oil on canvas, 110 x 110 cm
Österreichische Galerie, Vienna

Portrait of Adele Bloch-Bauer. 1907
Oil on canvas, 138 x 138 cm
Österreichische Galerie, Vienna

Danaë. 1907/08
Oil on canvas, 77 x 83 cm
Sammlung Dichand, Vienna

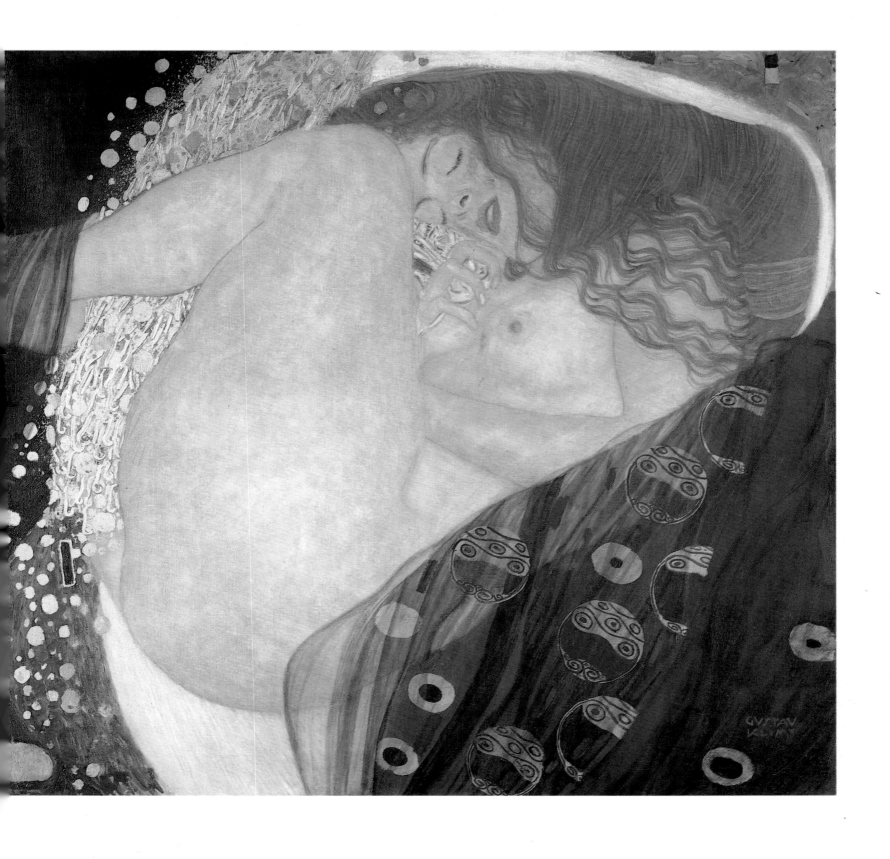

The Kiss. 1907/08
Oil on canvas, 180 x 180 cm
Österreichische Galerie, Vienna

Kammer Castle on the Atter Lake. 1908
Oil on canvas, 110 x 110 cm
Narodny Galerie, Prague

Expectation. 1905/09
Cardboard for the Stoclet frieze
Aquarelle/gouache on paper. 193 x 115 cm
Österr. Museum für angewandte Kunst, Vienna

Nachlaß meines Bruders Gustav

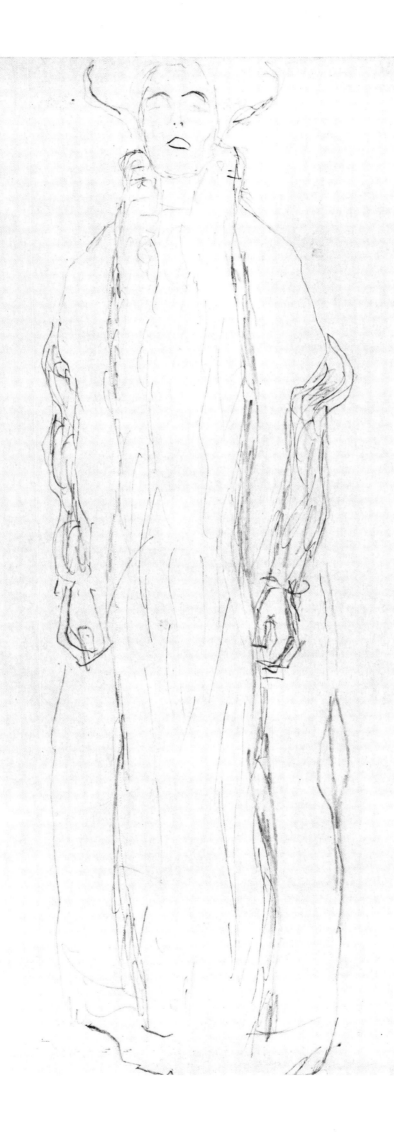

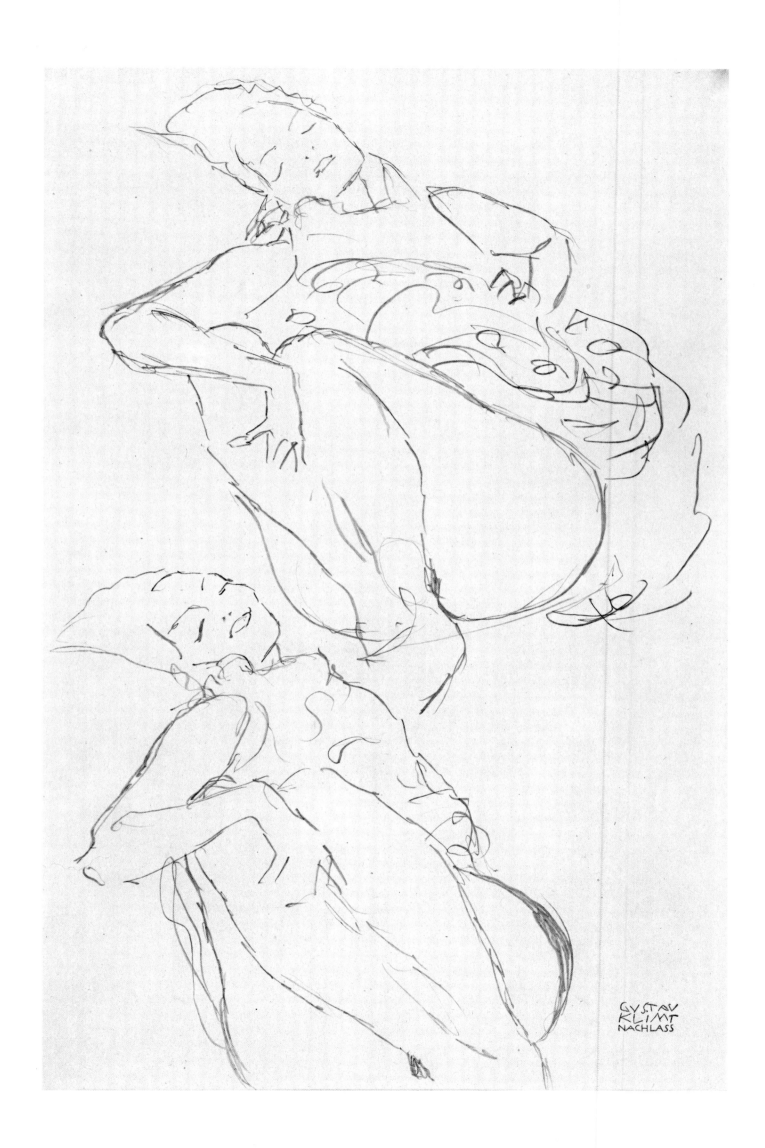

GVSTAV
KLIMT
NACHLASS

88

Fulfillment. 1905/09
Cardboard for the Stoclet frieze
Aquarelle/gouache on paper, 193 x 120 cm
Musée d'Art Moderne, Strasbourg

Woman with Hat and Feather Boa. 1909
Oil on canvas, 69 x 55 cm
Österreichische Galerie, Vienna

Judith II (Salome). 1909
Oil on canvas, 178 x 46 cm
Museo d'Arte Moderna, Venice

Black Feather Hat. 1910
Oil on canvas, 79 x 63 cm
Private collection

Adele Bloch-Bauer. 1912
Oil on canvas, 190 x 120 cm
Österreichische Galerie, Vienna

Avenue in the Park of Kammer Castle. 1912
Oil on canvas, 110 x 110 cm
Österreichische Galerie, Vienna

The Virgin. 1912/13
Oil on canvas, 190 x 200 cm
Narodny Galerie, Prague

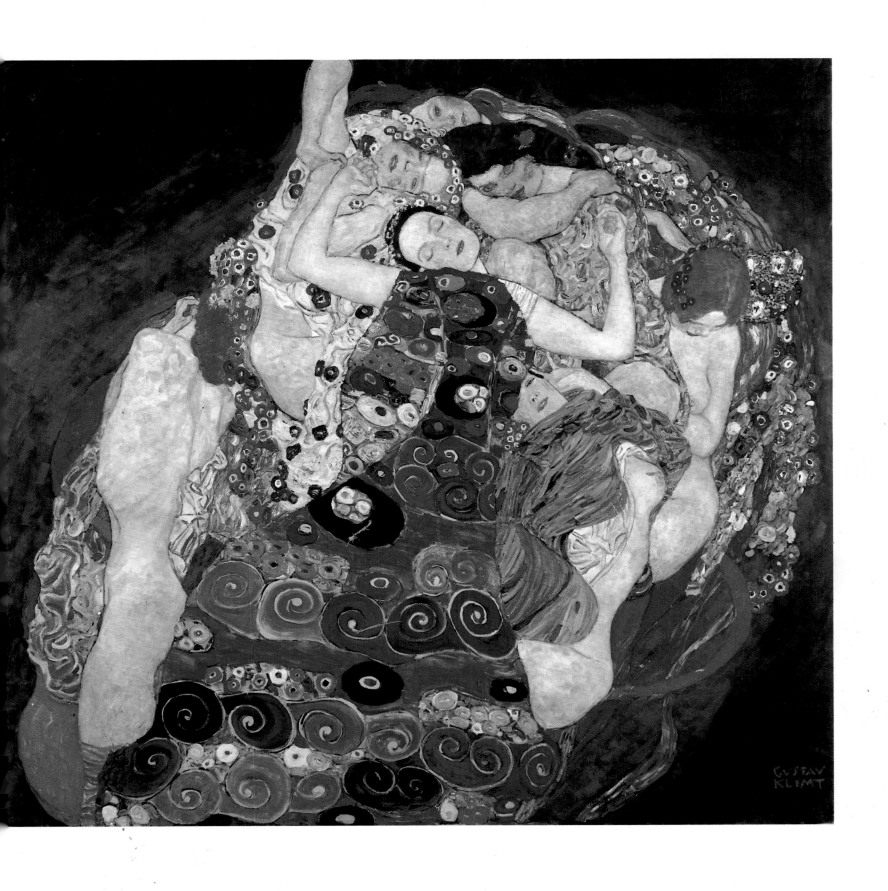

Unterach on the Atter Lake. 1915
Oil on canvas, 110 x 110 cm
Residenzgalerie, Salzburg

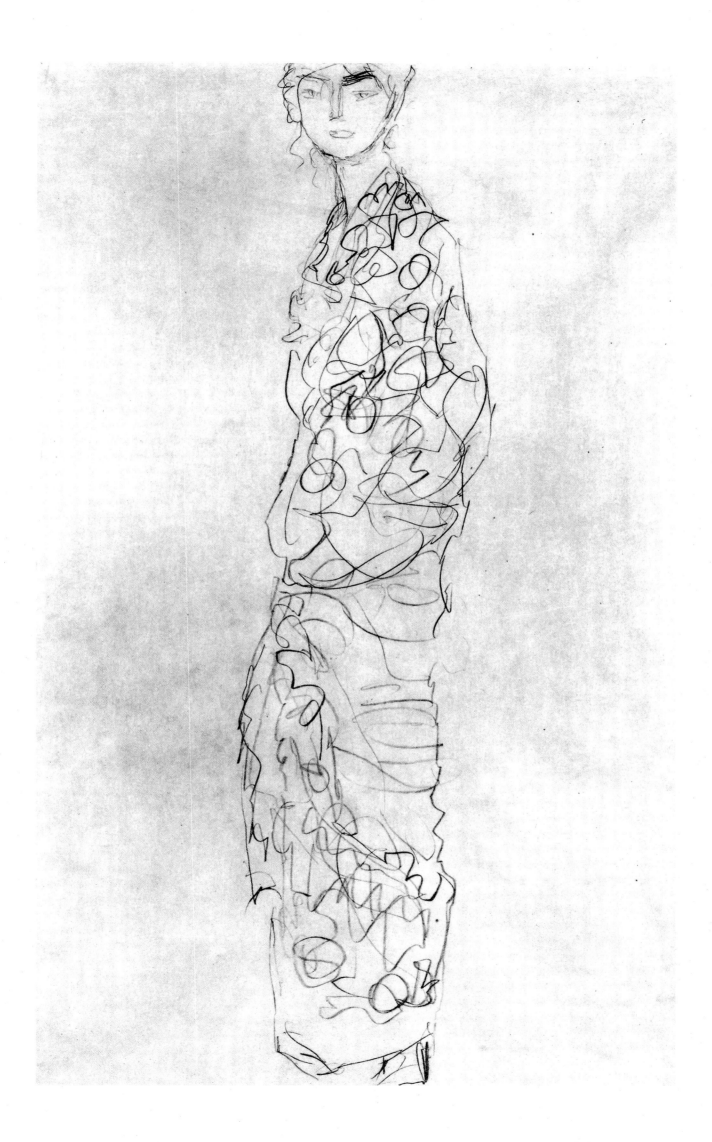

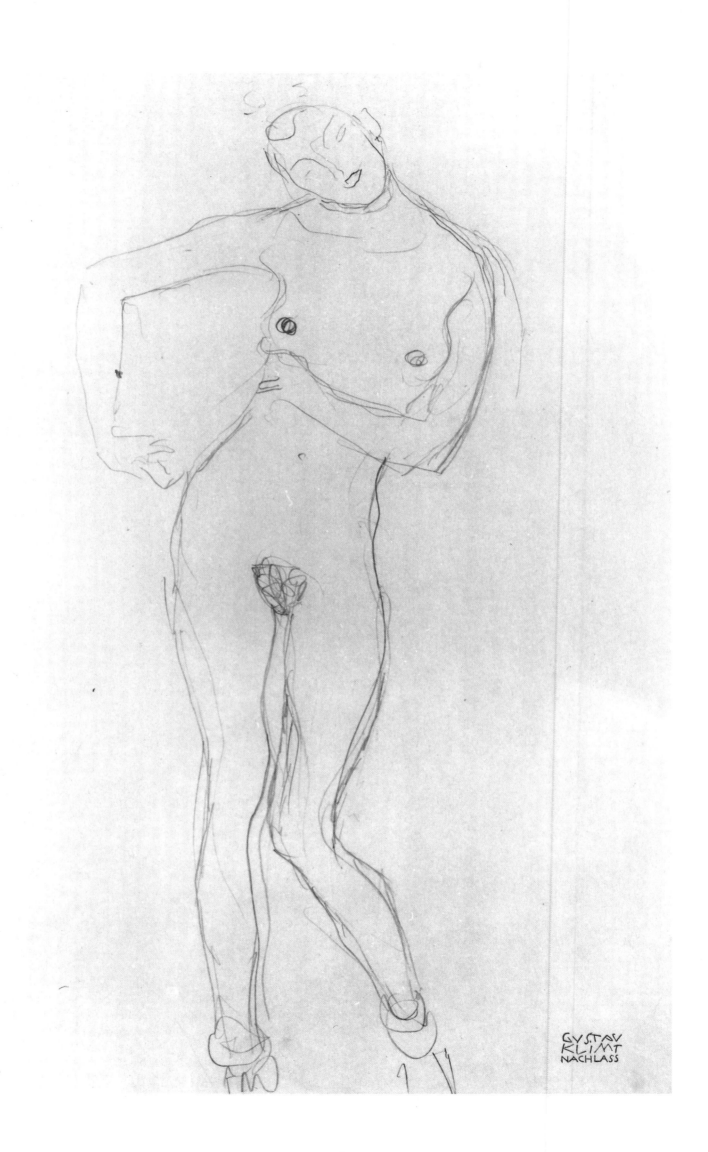

Portrait of Johanna Staude. 1917/18
Oil on canvas, 70 x 60 cm
Östereichische Galerie, Vienna

Adam and Eve. 1917/18
Oil on canvas, 173 x 60 cm
Österreichische Galerie, Vienna

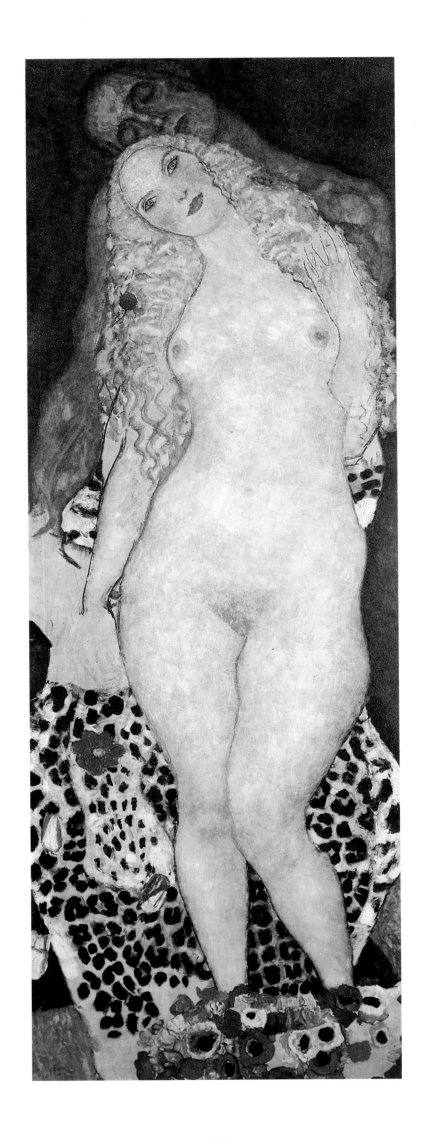

119

Portrait of a Woman. 1917/18
Oil on canvas, 180 x 90 cm
Neue Galerie der Stadt Linz,
Wolfgang-Gurlitt-Museum

Woman's Head. 1918
Oil on canvas, 67 x 56 cm
Neue Galerie der Stadt Linz,
Wolfgang-Gurlitt-Museum

TABLE OF ILLUSTRATIONS

THE LIBRARY
CITY AND EAST LONDON COLLEGE
JUBILEE STREET, E1 3HA

131

THE LIBRARY
TOWER HAMLETS COLLEGE
JUBILEE STREET
LONDON E1 3HA
TEL: 071 538 5888